MW01392643

WATCHMAN NEE

Ministering to the House or to God?

Living Stream Ministry
Anaheim, California

© 1993 Living Stream Ministry

All rights reserved. No part of this work may be reproduced or transmitted in any form or by any means—graphic, electronic, or mechanical, including photocopying, recording, or information storage and retrieval systems—without written permission from the publisher.

ISBN 1-57593-869-3

Living Stream Ministry

1853 W. Ball Road, Anaheim, CA 92804 USA
P. O. Box 2121, Anaheim, CA 92814 USA

97 98 99 00 01 / 9 8 7 6 5 4 3 2 1

MINISTERING TO THE HOUSE OR TO GOD?

Scripture Reading: Ezek. 44:9-26, 28, 31; Luke 17:7-10

These two portions of the Word show us two different attitudes that are displayed before God. Before we look into these matters using the Word with the shining of God's light, I want the brothers and sisters to know what are our responsibilities and what is God's continual focus in the church in this age.

Brothers and sisters, let me ask something very frankly. Are we really ministering to the believers or to Him? Is the focus of our work really on the work or on the Lord? There is a great difference. Ministering to the house is extremely different from ministering to Jesus Christ. We can see many today ministering and serving, but they are only in the outer court. They have not come near to the table. Oh, many are ministering to the house and not to the Lord. The ministering that the Lord is after—the ministering that He is continually after—is to minister to Him. His desire is not for us to do His work. Laboring is certainly important, plowing the fields is important, and feeding the cattle is also important, but the Lord does not look at these things. Rather, He is after the ministering to God and the serving of God. He wants His slaves to minister to Him and to serve Him. Oh, how happy are those who are able to minister to Him.

Now I want to mention the difference between these two kinds of ministering. Let us search these two portions of the Word. We are not here to expound the Scriptures. The expounding of the Scriptures has become the trap to many spiritual believers. There is really no matter that has so damaged the believers as the expounding of the Scriptures. I am speaking of the spiritual believers here. We always assume that as long as we can find two similar verses in the Scriptures, then we can expound them. No. There is no such thing! Today we will first learn a lesson and then study the lesson. Before we study the lesson, we must first learn the lesson and know how to minister to God. We must first meet the One who wrote the Book before we can read the words. We must first know Him before we can know His Book. If we put the Bible as the top priority, we are failures. Therefore, from the beginning we want to declare that we are not here to expound the Scriptures; rather, we are here to learn a lesson. As such we are using these two portions of the Word to proclaim what we should have experienced and what we have experienced.

Ezekiel 44:11, 15-16 says, "Yet they shall be ministers in my sanctuary, having charge at the gates of the house, and ministering to the house: they shall slay the burnt offering and the sacrifice for the people, and they shall stand before them to minister unto them....But the priests the Levites, the sons of Zadok, that kept the charge of my sanctuary when the children of Israel went astray from me, they shall come near to me to minister unto me, and they shall stand before me to offer unto me the fat and the blood, saith the Lord God: they shall enter into my sanctuary, and they shall come near to my table, to minister unto me, and they shall keep my charge." You see that verse 11 is very different from verses 15 and 16. There is a basic difference between them. Verse 11 speaks of ministering to the house. Verses 15 and 16 speak of ministering to "Me"—that is, the ministering to Jehovah. In Hebrew, the same word for ministering is used in both of these verses. According to God there were two groups of Levites. Although all were Levites belonging to God and to one tribe, the majority among them were only worthy to minister to the house. Yet there was a small minority, who were not only Levites but also the sons of Zadok, who could minister to "Me"—that is, minister to Jehovah.

Brothers and sisters, do you know what it is to minister to the house and what it is to minister to Jehovah? Do you know the difference between these two kinds of ministering? Many say that there is nothing better than ministering to the house! They seem to say, "You see me doing my best to make my work expand, to strive for the kingdom, to work in the Lord's name, to bear the responsibility to help the church, and to earnestly endeavor to be the slave of the brothers. I do my best to render help to the brothers and sisters. I rush about to different places so as to make the church flourish and the work prosper." Many feel that it would be wonderful if they could save sinners and ask them to join the church, thereby causing the church to grow in numbers. But I say this is merely ministering to the house. As far as God is concerned, besides this kind of ministering, there is another kind of ministering. In God's eyes, not only is there the ministry to the house; there is also a better ministry. We are not only ministering before the Lord but also to the Lord. Here there is not only the ministering in the house, but there is also the ministering before the table. We are not only ministering before the Lord; rather, we are ministering to the Lord. This is a very different matter. These two are extremely different from each other. There is no similarity between them.

If you know the difference here, you will see what the Lord is after and what He has always been seeking. Brothers and sisters, please do not be mistaken. To minister to the Lord does not mean that you neglect the house. Rather, what I am saying is that there is not only ministering to the house, but there is something deeper, which is ministering to the Lord.

There are many who only know how to minister to the house and not to the Lord.

Let me ask you a few questions. Brothers, what are you preaching the gospel for? You desire to help prosper the work, but what is that really for? You rush to different places to labor, but what is that really for? I especially want to speak to the brothers and sisters who are co-workers. What are you really doing here? Do you hope that more can hear the gospel? I only mention the good things. I will not mention those things which are of a lower standard. No doubt it is good to preach the gospel. It is also good to save the sinners and help the brothers and sisters make progress. No doubt you have done your best to be very faithful to preach and perfect. However, your eyes are only set on the brothers and sisters. This is ministering to the house. Since you are ministering before people, you are ministering to them and not to the Lord. This does not mean that those who minister to the Lord will not do these things. Those who minister to the Lord will also do these things, but their one goal is to be for the Lord. They treasure men absolutely for the Lord's sake. Hence, their focus is not only on men. If you come to the Lord's presence, focusing only on Him, you will spontaneously be able to minister to the brothers also. This is a big difference.

In the following sections, we will see the basic difference between ministering to the Lord and ministering to the house. Then we will see how to minister to the Lord and how to minister to the house. Finally, we will see the requirements of one who ministers to the Lord. These are three matters we will mention.

THE DIFFERENCE BETWEEN MINISTERING TO THE HOUSE AND MINISTERING TO THE LORD

We must see clearly that outwardly there may not be much difference between ministering to the house and ministering to the Lord. You may try your best to render help to the brothers, to diligently save the sinners, and to labor much in the service to manage the church. On top of these, you may do your best to admonish others to read the Bible and pray. You may have suffered much and have been persecuted. You may do everything. But there is a basic question: What is your motivation for doing this? The question hinges on whether or not the Lord occupies the first place in your heart. When you rise up early in the morning to minister to the brothers and sisters, do you say, "O Lord, today I am doing this once again for Your sake"? Or do you first remember that this is your duty, and you do it because this is what you should do? If this is the case, it is altogether out of necessity, and it is not for the Lord. You only saw your brothers; you did not see the Lord. Your motive tells everything about your situation. Your situation hinges on why you do things.

Let me tell you very frankly: the work has areas that are appealing to the flesh. Brothers, let us take, for example, a person who is active by nature. It is his nature to speak a great deal. If you ask him to go to the countryside to preach the gospel, run to and fro from one village to another, and speak here and there, he is very happy. Why do you think he does this? He is basically an active person who loves to speak. I can tell you frankly that he is not doing this for the Lord because many times he is not able to do the things he does not like, even though the Lord really wants him to. According to his nature, he likes to preach the gospel; so he is happy to do it and feels that he is ministering to the Lord. Actually, he is ministering to the house. Brothers and sisters, there is a big difference here! In the Lord's work there are areas which are interesting, adventurous, and attractive to the flesh! When you give messages, many flock to hear you. When you read a portion of the Bible, everyone comments that you have done a good job. When you preach the gospel, many are saved through you. This is really lovely and appealing to you. Just consider how interesting this is.

If I am doing housework, busying myself from morning till evening; if I am a worker in a factory, listening to the sound of machines from morning till evening; if I am an office worker, handling papers and letters from morning till evening; or if I am someone's maid, cleaning tables, mopping floors, and cooking for others from morning till evening, I might consider this to be meaningless! But if I could be free from these things to do the Lord's work, how good it would be! A sister may think it is dull to stay home and take care of the children, to be someone's wife, and to do all the household chores! If she could be set free to speak of spiritual things here and speak of the Lord's things there, how good it would be! But this is the attraction of the flesh and is not spiritual. It is solely for the pleasure of the self.

Oh, may we see that much of the labor and ministering before God is not ministering to Him. The Bible tells us that there was a group of Levites who were busily ministering in the house, but they were only ministering to the house, not to God. Ministering to the house is very similar to ministering to the Lord. Outwardly, there is almost no difference. Those Levites were in the house preparing the peace offerings and burnt offerings. This was a wonderful work. Suppose an Israelite wanted to worship God and offer up a peace offering and burnt offering, but he could not drag in the cattle or sheep. The Levites would help him drag in the animals and slay them. How good this was! They helped someone else be close to the Lord and know the Lord! Even today, it is a wonderful work to lead a sinner to turn or help a believer advance. While the Levites worked, they were very busy and their whole body was sweating. They helped others to carry out the offering of the cattle and sheep. Both the peace offering and burnt offering typify Christ.

This means that they exerted their energy to bring others to the Lord. It is so wonderful that some could be brought to know the Lord. We know that the peace offering concerns the relationship between a sinner and the Lord, and the burnt offering concerns the relationship between a believer and the Lord. The peace offering speaks of a sinner's drawing near to the Lord, while the burnt offering speaks of the consecration of a believer. In the Levites' work, not only were sinners brought to believe in the Lord, but believers were also brought to consecrate themselves. How wonderful this work was. This was not a false work; it was altogether genuine. God knew their work. They were truly rendering help to others in offering up the peace offerings and burnt offerings. They were truly saving and helping men; they labored very hard. Nevertheless, God said they were not ministering to Him.

Brothers and sisters, please remember that ministering to the Lord is much deeper than leading men to the Lord. Ministering to the Lord is also much deeper than leading believers to consecrate themselves to the Lord. Ministering to the Lord is one step further than leading men to the Lord and leading believers to consecrate themselves to the Lord. In God's eyes, leading men to the Lord and leading believers to consecrate themselves to the Lord are merely ministering to the house. Ministering to the Lord is something deeper. What do you see before God? Do you only see the need for the salvation of sinners? Do you only see the need to render help for the progress of believers? Or do you see something deeper? I am not here to save sinners; neither am I here to render help to believers. Can you say this? I fear very much that many would say, "If saving sinners and rendering help to the believers is not my work, what shall I do? I will have nothing to do." Friends, besides these, do you have other work? Oh, with many this is all they have. Many say, "If I did not do the work of helping and saving others, what would I do?" Apart from these things, they have nothing to do. Their work is confined to the house. If you take away these things, they will have nothing left to do.

Brothers and sisters, if you knew the heavy burden within me, you would know the goal of God. God is not after the outward, lively ministering. God is not after the salvation of sinners. God is not after gaining men or helping believers to be more spiritual or more advanced. God has only one goal: to have men belong absolutely to "Me." In other words, He wants us to be before "My" presence and minister to "Me." God's unique goal is not in so many things. Rather, it is in "Me."

I say again, I am not afraid of bothering people. What I fear most in my heart is that many will come out to preach the gospel to help men, save sinners, and perfect the believers, yet not minister to the Lord! The goal of many so-called ministries to the Lord is none other than serving their own likes and pleasures. It is unbearable for them to be confined. They are energetic and must run around and be active in order to be happy! Although outwardly they are ministering to sinners and the brothers, inwardly they are ministering to their flesh! If they do not do this, they are not happy. Truly they are altogether not after the Lord's pleasure. It seems that I am giving you a hard time, but this is the truth. Please remember, there are many areas in the Lord's work that naturally attract us. However, this is truly damaging to us. When we see something naturally attractive in the Lord's work, we go about doing it! What a pity this is! For this reason, we must pray to God to grace us that we may know what it is to minister to God and to the house.

I have a very dear friend who is already on the other side of the veil. She belonged to the Lord, and I loved her very much in the Lord. One day the two of us were praying on a mountain, and afterward we read the portion of the Word in Ezekiel 44. She was much older than I, so she said, "Little brother, twenty years ago I read this portion of the Bible." I asked her how she had felt after reading it. She said, "When I came to this passage, I immediately closed the Bible, knelt down, and prayed, 'Lord, let me minister to You. Do not let me minister to the house.'" Brothers and sisters, I have not forgotten this incident, and I will never forget it. Although she has passed away, I remember her words all the time, "Lord, let me minister to You. Do not let me minister to the house." Can we pray such a prayer, saying, "Lord, I want minister to You; I do not want to minister to the house"?

I fear very much that many lust for something of God yet do not want God

Himself. Many think that saving souls is the most important thing, and they would give up their jobs to do this. The married sisters do not want to take care of the housework, the single sisters give up their consideration of marriage, and those who have a job do not want to work. They think that it is meaningless to continue doing what they are doing. They consider it irksome to work, take care of the family, serve, and study. They think that it would be wonderful if they could be released to preach the gospel. But friends, there are only two questions: Are you ministering to God? Or are you ministering to the house?

HOW TO MINISTER TO THE HOUSE AND HOW TO MINISTER TO THE LORD

Many like to exercise their muscles outside because by killing cattle and sheep, they can exercise their strength and fleshly energy. However, if you ask them to go to a quiet, solitary place where no one can see them, they are not able to do this. The sanctuary is an extremely dim place. Within there are only seven olive oil lamps which may not be as bright as seven candles! Many consider that ministering to the Lord in the sanctuary is not that interesting. But this is the place where the Lord wants us to be. Here it is calm and dark, and there are no crowds or great multitudes of people. Yet here one finds the genuine ministry to the Lord. Brothers, we cannot find a genuine servant of God or true minister to the Lord who does not minister in this way.

Now let us consider what the Levites were doing. They were killing cattle and sheep outside the house. Men can see you in such a place; the work is very apparent. Others will praise you, saying that you are wonderful and strong because you have killed many cattle and sheep and tied them to the altar. Many people are thrilled at the outward achievements of the work.

But what is involved in ministering to the Lord? Verse 15 says very clearly, "But the priests the Levites, the sons of Zadok, that kept the charge of my sanctuary when the children of Israel went astray from me, they shall come near to me to minister unto me, and they shall stand before me to offer unto me the fat and the blood, saith the Lord God." The basis for the ministry to the Lord, the basic requirement for ministering to the Lord, is to draw near to the Lord. It is to be bold enough to come before Him, to sit firmly before Him, and to stand before Him. Brothers, do we know how to draw near to the Lord? How often we find that we have to drag ourselves into His presence! Many indeed are fearful of being left alone in a dark room. They are afraid of being alone and cannot stand being shut in by themselves. Many times even though they are in a room, their heart is wandering outside, and they can no longer come near to the Lord. They cannot be alone by themselves and quietly learn to pray before Him. Many are very happy to work, join the crowd, and even preach to men. But how many can really draw near to God in the Holy of Holies? Many cannot draw near to God in that dim, quiet, and solitary sanctuary. However, no one can minister to Him without drawing near to Him. No one can minister to the Lord without approaching Him in prayer. Spiritual power is not the power of preaching but the power of praying. How much you pray indicates how much inner strength you really possess. No spiritual matter requires more strength than prayer. It is possible to read the Bible without exerting much effort. I am not saying that there is no effort involved in reading the Bible, but this is something that is rather easy to achieve. It is possible to preach the gospel without much effort, and it is possible to render help to the brothers without exerting much spiritual strength. In speaking, it is possible for one to rely on his memory to do the job. But in order to come to God and kneel before Him for an hour, there is the need for one to exert the strength of his whole being. Indeed, if one does not strive in such a way, he will not be able to maintain such a work; he will not be able to persevere. Every minister of the Lord knows the preciousness of such times: the sweetness of waking at midnight and spending an hour in prayer before going back to sleep, and the wonderful feeling of rising up very early in the morning for an hour's prayer. Unless we draw near to God, we cannot minister to Him. It is impossible to minister to the Lord and stand afar off at the same time. The disciples could follow the Lord from a far distance, but none of those who followed in that way could minister to Him. It is possible to follow the Lord secretly at a distance, but it is impossible to minister to Him in such a way. The sanctuary is the unique place where ministry to Him is possible. You can approach the people in the outer court, but you can approach God only in the sanctuary. Actually, those who can render help to the church and can do something are those who are near to God. If the labor before God is merely for the brothers and sisters, how poor the work will be.

If we want to minister to the Lord, we must draw near to Him. What should our condition be before God? "They shall stand before me" (v. 15). It seems to me that we always want to be on the go, as if standing still were an impossible thing to do. We cannot stand still. Many brothers and sisters are extremely busy. There are many things before them, and they feel that they have to keep going. If you ask them to stand still and wait for awhile, they will not be able to do it. But all spiritual persons know what it is to stand before God.

What does it mean to stand? It means to wait for a command, to wait upon the Lord to speak His will. Countless numbers of works have been set up. I am not speaking of the work in factories and offices. Christians ought to be absolutely faithful to their earthly masters. We have to be very faithful in serving our earthly masters. But when it comes to spiritual work, we need to be more than just efficient. I speak in particular to all the co-workers. Brothers, is your work fully set? Is your work carried out efficiently? Can you not stand still and wait for awhile? Has much of your work been arranged and listed in order? Do you methodically work according to the list? Are you complete in everything? Brothers, can you wait for another three days? Can you stand still for a moment and not move around? This is to stand before the Lord. Everyone who does not know how to draw near to the Lord will surely not be able to minister to Him. Similarly, everyone who does not know how to stand before the Lord will surely not be able to minister to Him. It is impossible for them to minister to the Lord. Brothers, should not a servant wait for an order before he does anything?

Let me reiterate. Since this is a spiritual matter, I am not afraid of repetition. There are only two types of sin before God. One is rebellion against His command. If He gives an order and you refuse to do it, it is sin. But there is another type of sin, which is doing something without the Lord's command. One is the sin of rebellion, and the other is the sin of presumption. One ignores what the Lord has said; the other does what the Lord has not said. Standing before the Lord is the way to deal with the sin of doing what the Lord has not commanded. Brothers and sisters, how much of your spiritual work is done only after you are clear about God's will? How many really work as a result of the Lord's charge? Perhaps you work out of your zeal or because you consider it a good thing to do. Let me tell you that nothing damages God's will more than good things. Good things hinder God the most. We can easily recognize that as Christians we should not take part in evil, unclean, and lustful things and that these things are intolerable. Thus, it is unlikely for these things to be a hindrance to God's purpose. The things that hinder God's purpose are the good things, the things that are similar to His purpose. We may think that such a thing is not bad or that there is nothing better, and we may do it without asking if it is the Lord's will. Good things are God's greatest enemy. Indeed, every time we rebel against God, it is because we presume that something is good, and we go ahead and do it. As children of God, we all know that we cannot sin and that we should not do evil. But how often have we done something just because there was no conviction from the conscience or because the conscience thought it is all right to do?

No doubt, such a thing may be very good. But have we stood before the Lord? We need to stand before Him. Standing means to not walk or move; it means to remain in a place, to stand still and wait for the Lord's order. Brothers, this is the ministry to the Lord. The killing of cattle and sheep in the outer court is done whenever someone comes to offer a sacrifice. But in the Holy of Holies, there is utter solitude and no man in sight. In the Holy of Holies, no brother or sister has any authority over us, neither will a conference make decisions for us, nor does a committee have the authority to commission us. In the Holy of Holies, there is only one authority that will govern us, and that is the Lord. We will only do what the Lord directs us to do; otherwise, we will not do anything. Brothers, can we really stand before Him?

If we want to minister to the Lord in

the Holy of Holies, we must spend time before the Lord and pray more. Otherwise, we will be inadequate. We need to pray to be ushered into God's presence and to draw near to Him. Hence, to pray is to stand before God; it is to seek His will before Him. Thank the Lord that although every believer does not do this, some are standing before the Lord and following Him in the journey ahead.

In order to stand before the Lord, it is necessary "to offer unto me the fat and the blood" (Ezek. 44:15). We know that God is holy and righteous in the Holy Place and that God is glorious in the Holy of Holies. God's glory fills the Holy of Holies; God's holiness and righteousness fill the Holy Place. The blood is for God's holiness and righteousness, while the fat is for His glory. The fat is for God to gain something, while the blood deals with God's holiness and righteousness. We all know that God is holy and righteous and that He absolutely cannot accept anyone sinful. Without the shedding of blood or the remission of sin, without man paying a price for his sin, God will never be satisfied. Therefore, there is the need for the blood. There is no way to approach

God without it. In the Old Testament time, man was put aside and could not come forward to God. But we can come before God because we have the Lord's blood. Not only so, but we also have to offer the fat, which means to offer the richest and best. We know that the blood deals with sin. But the fat is for God's satisfaction. The fat is the richest and best part, and it satisfies God's heart. Thus, it is for God's glory.

All those who would come before God to minister to Him must answer to God's holiness, righteousness, and even His glory. The entire Bible, both the Old Testament and the New Testament, focuses on these three things: God's holiness, God's righteousness, and God's glory. God's glory refers to God Himself; God's holiness refers to His nature; and God's righteousness refers to His way. In other words, God's way is righteous, God's nature is holy, and God Himself is glory. Every time we come before God, we must first realize how we are able to stand before God. God is holy and righteous! How can sinners like us meet Him? We can meet Him because the blood is here, remitting and cleansing us from our sin. As a result, we can approach God without any conflict because His blood has cleansed us from all unrighteousness. However, He is not only holy and righteous; He is also glorious in Himself. Therefore, there is a need to offer the fat, which is to offer up our very best to God for His satisfaction. In other words, the blood deals with everything in the old creation, and the fat speaks of everything in the new creation. The blood dispels everything of the old creation, so that we no longer have a problem concerning holiness and righteousness. The fat is of the new creation, which signifies the offering of ourselves to God, so that we no longer have a problem with God's glory.

We cannot minister to God if we do not know death and resurrection. Death is not a doctrine or a theory from the Bible; it is poured out through a genuine trust in Him and in the pouring out of His incorruptible blood. When His incorruptible blood was poured out, we too were poured out. Thank the Lord. Now our Lord has no blood. He only has a body with bones and flesh. Everything of the natural life was poured out. When the Lord's blood was poured out, everything of the soul-life was poured out. He indeed poured out His soul unto death (Isa. 53:12). This is the significance of the blood. The pouring out of the blood is the removal of everything natural. (We will speak more concerning this matter later.)

If we want to minister before God, we need to draw near to Him, stand before Him, and wait for His will. Please remember these two indispensable matters. On the one hand, we must continually pour out "our blood"—we must continually acknowledge that everything we have by birth and lose by death has been poured out. Many frequently ask me what the natural life really is. I often answer them by saying that everything that comes with birth and goes with death is of the natural life; everything that exists between birth and death is the natural life. Praise the Lord! He has already poured out everything of our natural life. In other words, He has poured out everything that we obtained and everything that came by birth. When the Lord poured out His blood, He did not only pour out His own life, but ours as well. Hence, we have to continually stand on this fact and deny our soul-life. Brothers and sisters, this is altogether not a doctrine but a reality. Everything of the natural life is thus dropped before God.

Brothers and sisters, this is a goal that we can attain to because, in Christ, everything of the soul has been poured out so that it is now possible for us to be selfless. Thank the Lord, we can be selfless because Christ poured out our self when He poured out His blood. By ourselves, this is impossible; we cannot crucify ourselves. Thank the Lord that the Son of God has accomplished this fact. By Him we can die, and by Him we can give up our self. But it is not sufficient just to die, because death is only the negative side. Our focus before God is not only on death but also on resurrection. When He arose, we were in Him. In Him, we became a new creation. He not only died but also rose from the dead. He lives unto God; therefore, all that He is, is for God's satisfaction and not for Himself. Brothers and sisters, this is what God wants to show us. This is what it is to minister to the Lord. We must offer Him the fat and the blood.

Verse 16 says, "They shall enter into my sanctuary, and they shall come near to my table, to minister unto me, and they shall keep my charge." This verse tells us that there is a place to minister to the Lord. The ministry to the Lord is in the sanctuary—a hidden, quiet place not public like the outer court. Brothers and sisters, may He grace us so that we would not consider it a suffering to be in the sanctuary. Actually, a day there is better than a thousand days in another place. Yet we are always afraid of the sanctuary. How good it is to be in the outer court! Everyone can see us there. How good it is to be in the outer court! They all know us there. How good it is to be in the outer court! Our names are well known, and there is no attack or slander there, only a welcome and praises. How wonderful this is! But God wants us to be in the sanctuary. When we are in that place, others may say that we are lazy and not doing anything. In reality, what is done there is far superior to the work of ministering to the people in the outer court. Have you heard others criticizing you for being small and narrow? Have you heard others say that you will not do this or that? Others may say that you are too lazy to work and that you have left many things undone. But brothers and sisters, our hearts are not narrow at all. We are not asking anything of men, and we do not want to stand at the gate for many to see. We have only one goal, which is to minister to the Lord in the Holy Place. Brothers and sisters, we are not willing to minister in the house because our hope and our task are greater than this. No one here is as ambitious as Paul was. He had one ambition, which was to please the Lord. The things we are seeking here are greater than many other things, and our labor here is greater than that of many who do great works. The fact is that our heart is broader than anyone else's. Brothers, do not think that we are too small and narrow. We are very broad, for we are not only ministering to the house but to the Lord as well. Of course this is not that great in the sight of man. Brothers and sisters, we would rather let others criticize us than to move without God's will. We have only two positions here: one is that we are dead and have dropped everything of the old creation; the other is that we are resurrected and are serving God, learning to stand before Him, listening to His order, and waiting in His presence to minister to Him. We do not care for anything else. O brothers and sisters, is God's will enough to satisfy you? Is it enough to do His will? Is His will good enough? Or are you still pursuing other things? Are all of God's plans for you good enough? Oh, you must learn to minister to God in His presence.

Since time is so short and we also have to cover Luke 17, I cannot share in more detail. I have said earlier that I wanted to mention three things. One is the difference between ministering to the house and ministering to the Lord; another is the way to minister to the house and the way to minister to the Lord; and the third is the requirements and condition of one who ministers to the Lord. Now let us consider the requirements of one who ministers to the Lord.

THE REQUIREMENTS OF ONE WHO MINISTERS TO THE LORD

Those who ministered to God before Him had to be clothed with linen garments, linen bonnets on their heads, and linen breeches on their loins. Their whole body was clothed with linen material. Verse 17 also says that no wool should come upon them. No one who ministered to the Lord could be clothed with wool. Before God, no one could ever put on woolen garments. Why? Please read Ezekiel 44:18: "They shall have linen bonnets upon their heads, and shall have linen breeches upon their loins; they shall not gird themselves with any thing that causeth sweat." This portion of the Word reveals that all those who minister to the Lord should not sweat. All work that produces sweat is not pleasing to God and is rejected by Him. What is the meaning of sweat? The first sweat in the entire world was shed by Adam when he was driven out of the garden of Eden. Genesis 3 tells us that, due to Adam's sin, God punished him by saying, "In the sweat of thy face shalt thou eat bread." Sweat is a result of the curse. Due to God's curse, the ground ceased to yield its fruit; due to the absence of God's blessing, human effort is necessary, and this causes sweat. What is the work that causes sweat? It is the work that comes out of human effort without the blessing from God the Father. Everyone ministering to God should absolutely abstain from any work that causes sweat. Numerous works placed before God require effort and running around for their accomplishment. Everyone ministering to God must do a work that causes no sweat. All of God's work is serene; it is not accomplished by running around but by sitting down. Although outwardly one may be very busy, he is very restful within; although outwardly it is hot, within it is very calm. This work is done by sitting down. This is the work that causes no sweat! All the real work before God is not accidental and not accomplished by fleshly effort. Unfortunately, so much of today's work cannot be accomplished without sweating. What a pity that today's work cannot be accomplished unless someone is planning, sponsoring, promoting, proposing, running around, admonishing, exhorting, and exerting human effort and fleshly strength. Oh, it is really a pity that in most cases, without sweat, there is no work. Please bear in mind that sweating outside is permissible. In slaying cattle and sheep outside, serving sinners, and ministering to the saints, sweating is permissible. If you are doing that kind of work, you can sweat all you want. But those who minister to the Lord in the Holy Place absolutely cannot sweat. God does not need man's sweating. No doubt, all work is busy, but God's work does not need fleshly strength. I do not mean that there is no need of spiritual strength. In fact, how much spiritual strength you need and how much suffering you have to go through is hard to say. No one cares to distinguish between spiritual work and fleshly work. Men conclude that all of God's work cannot be accomplished without running around, spending time to discuss and debate, negotiating, proposing, approving, and authorizing. Yet if you ask them to wait quietly before God and listen to His speaking, they cannot do it because the flesh is not capable of doing this. Oh, all these require sweating.

The most important aspect of spiritual work is to deal with God. The first person we should contact is God, not man. The work of the flesh is different; the first one it contacts is man. Hence, if a work cannot be accomplished without man, it is not the work of God. How precious it is to be in God's presence. We have to deal with Him alone. We are not idle; rather, we are doing a work that causes no sweat. What does this mean? If we deal properly with God, there is no need to sweat before man. We can accomplish the most amount of work with the least amount of strength. The reason there are so many advertisements, promotions, and proposals is because men are not praying before God. Let me say that all spiritual work is done only before God.

If we take care of our work properly before God, we will not need many ways. Others will spontaneously respond to us and spontaneously profit. God is working, and there is no need of human strength and sweating.

Brothers and sisters, we should examine ourselves very honestly before God. Let us ask Him, "O Lord, am I really ministering to You or to the work? O Lord, is my ministry unto the house or unto You?" If we are sweating from morning till evening, then we can surely say to ourselves that we are ministering to the house and not to the Lord. If all our business and laboring are to meet outward needs, we can conclude that we are ministering to people and not to God. I do not despise such people, for they also are doing God's work. There is a need for some to slay the cattle and sheep. There is a need for some to lead and guide others. The children of Israel needed some to minister to them. But God desires something much deeper. We ought to pray to Him, "O God! I beg You to deliver me that I might not fall into the realm of ministering to the people." There is more than just ministering to the people. Brothers and sisters, too many are already ministering to the people. Why do we still want to add our portion there? God has no way to demand everyone to minister to Him; God cannot do this since many are not willing to minister to Him. Because man is not willing, it is impossible to revive the whole church and cause everyone to become faithful. Many are truly saved and have God's life, yet they just want to minister to the people. There is no way to change them because they do not want to miss the excitement on the outside. They will not let go of the work on the outside; their focus is on the field of work. Surely, there are some who need to take care of these matters. But the question is, are we among those taking part in these things? I hope we all can say to the Lord, "O God, I want to minister to You. I am willing to drop everything, to let go of all the work and forsake all the outward things. I want to minister to You and do a spiritual work. I am willing to give up all the outward things. I want to enter within, more deeply within."

There was no way for God to ask all the Levites to come. He could only choose the sons of Zadok. Why? Because when the children of Israel turned against the ways of the Lord and forsook Him, the sons of Zadok kept the charge of the sanctuary. They saw that what was on the outside was beyond repair; what was on the outside had collapsed and was contaminated. So they left what was on the outside and concentrated on keeping the sanctuary holy. Brothers and sisters, can you let what is on the outside collapse? Perhaps you will use wood to support it, so that the structure will not collapse. But the Lord will say, "I do not care for these things. I will only preserve My sanctuary and reserve a place that is holy for My children." There is the need of a place to be wholly separated and sanctified to Him; a place where one can discern between what is proper and what is improper. God wants to preserve His sanctuary. What is on the outside is collapsing, and God has no way but to let it go. Since the sons of Zadok did what they did, God chose them. Truly, God has no way to deal with everyone, but He wants to deal with you! If you are not willing to let go of everything on the outside, to whom can God go? Brothers and sisters, I stand in the presence of God to beg you all; God is seeking those who will fully minister to

Him. There are really too many who are working on the outside. Those who are ministering to God on the inside are far too few. This is why God is crying, "Who will minister to Me in My sanctuary?"

Oh! I cannot say too much about this matter. I can only say that I very much enjoy reading Acts 13: "Now there were in Antioch, in the local church, prophets and teachers....And as they were ministering to the Lord and fasting, the Holy Spirit said, Set apart for Me now Barnabas and Saul for the work to which I have called them" (vv. 1-2). Such is the work of the New Testament. It is also the unique principle for the work of the New Testament. The work of the Holy Spirit can only be revealed at the time of ministering to the Lord. Only at the time of ministering to the Lord will the Holy Spirit send some forth. If we do not place ministering to the Lord as the top priority, everything will be out of order.

The work of the church in Antioch began during the time of ministering to the Lord. The Holy Spirit said, "Set apart for Me now Barnabas and Saul for the work to which I have called them." I repeat again, God does not want men to volunteer for His army. The soldiers who volunteer for the army are not wanted by God. God only has conscripted, or drafted, soldiers. We know that there are two kinds of soldiers in an army: one kind volunteer to join the army, and the other kind are drafted by the country. Based on the orders of the country, they have no choice except to serve as soldiers. But in the Lord's work, there are only drafted soldiers; there are no voluntary soldiers. Therefore, no one can say, because of his preference, he will go and preach the gospel; God will not use him. God's work has been greatly damaged by too many volunteer soldiers. They cannot declare as the Lord has declared, "Him who sent Me..." O brothers and sisters, this is not a light matter. God's work cannot be accomplished according to our will. God's work is completely His. We must check to see if this work is out of ourselves or out of the Lord's call. We must ask ourselves if we have volunteered to join the army or if we have been drafted by God. All the volunteer soldiers will not last; all those who recommended themselves will not last because God only wants soldiers who have been drafted by Him. When they ministered to the Lord, Paul and Barnabas did not say, "We will go forth to spread the gospel." Rather, the Holy Spirit said, *"Set apart for Me* now Barnabas and Saul for the work to which *I have called* them." Only the Holy Spirit has the authority to commission men to work. Concerning this matter, the church has no authority at all. Yet within many missionary societies and crusades there is the sending forth of men by men. God never allows such things. We should only minister to the Lord, not to the house. God desires to have those who will minister to Him directly and receive the commission by the Holy Spirit directly.

I say again, to minister to the Lord is not to forsake all the work on the outside. To minister to the Lord is not to give up serving in the villages. What I say is that all the work on the outside should be based on our ministry to the Lord. We go forth, out from our ministry to the Lord, rather than out from our own desires, which have no basis in the ministry to the Lord. There is a vast difference between these two matters. The difference is greater than that between heaven and earth. All those with experience realize that there is no difference greater than the difference between ministering to the Lord and ministering to the house.

It is one thing to know about the veil; we should minister to the Lord in the sanctuary. But beyond the veil, there is another matter which is just as important: "Let us therefore go forth unto Him outside the camp, bearing His reproach" (Heb. 13:13). The central thought of the book of Hebrews comprises these two things: the veil and the camp. Not only do we need to minister to God in the sanctuary, but we also need to go outside the camp. It is only when we have left the camp to minister to the Lord that He will speak and lead; at other times, He will not speak.

Let us now take a look at what Luke says. Let us clarify this once again: we do not want to expound on Luke. Rather, we want to find out from this portion of the Word what the Lord really wants. Luke 17:7-10 tells us very clearly that the Lord is satisfied with nothing other than Himself. He does not want you and me; He wants Himself. It is amazing that although the words here are quite severe, everyone feels that this portion is precious. There are two kinds of work here: one is plowing, or we may say, sowing. The other is the shepherding, or we may say, feeding. The work of sowing deals with those not yet regenerated. The work of shepherding deals with those who possess the life of God. Consequently, one kind of work concerns sinners, and the other kind of work concerns believers. These works cause those who have not received the Lord to receive the Lord and those who have received the Lord to be fed. Such is the work of the Lord's servants. This is also what we should do in the presence of God. This work is vital, and we must do our best. But the Lord is very amazing here. He said, "But which of you, having a slave who is plowing or tending sheep, will say to him when he has come in from the field, Come immediately and recline at table?" (Luke 17:7). This means that He would not do it this way. In other words, the servants, the Christians, should not be given food to eat after their work is done. Fleshly ones will say, "What a harsh Employer! We are extremely tired from plowing and feeding the cattle outside. Now that we are home, You should serve us food." But the Lord is not like a worldly master. (A different relationship between the earthly master and the servant is mentioned in Colossians and Ephesians. What is spoken of here is the treatment the Lord expects toward Himself. This is about the relationship between the spiritual master and the servant.) The Lord does not invite us to eat. What does He want then? Verse 8 says, "Will he not rather say to him"—that is, surely he will say to him—"Prepare something that I may dine, and gird yourself and serve me." This is what the Lord is doing. We always think to ourselves, "Today I have plowed so many acres of land and sown so many pounds of seeds. After so many days, so many months, there will be at least a thirty or sixty-fold harvest. Today I led so many sheep to the green pastures, to a certain spot in a certain place, and they drank beside the still waters. After so much time, these sheep will surely grow big and fat. This is indeed the greatest work. The produce from the land may serve as food; the products from the flock of sheep may serve as clothing." We are glad and enjoy the happiness from our labor. The meaning of eating and drinking is the enjoyment that comes out of our recollection of the work we have done. How often, after we have made some proud achievements, do we think about them even while we are sleeping and relish them in our memory. We may even think about them while we are eating and feel very proud and satisfied. Often we call to mind something and are thrilled by such thoughts. But the Lord said His goal for all the work, whether it be feeding the cattle or plowing the field, is not to make us happy, give us enjoyment, or let us have some gain. The Lord will surely say to us, "Prepare something that I may dine, and gird yourself and serve Me." Do we see this? What the Lord demands is that we minister to Him. Please remember that the work in the fields cannot be compared to the work at home. Please remember that the land and the cattle cannot be compared to the Lord. The Lord does not say here, "Since you labored so hard, plowed so much land, and fed so many cattle, you need not serve Me anymore; you may go to eat, drink and be merry." The Lord's words inform us how He weighs the importance of our labor and our need to minister to Him. He will not let us go just because we have plowed the land, fed the cattle, and done so much work on the outside; he will not tell us that there is no need to minister to Him. The Lord will not do this. He will by no means do this. He will not allow us to omit the ministering to Him just because we are too occupied with our work. He will not allow the hardship of the labor to rob Him of our ministry to Him. The first priority is to minister to the Lord because ministering to the Lord is more vital than all the plowing, feeding, and working.

Brothers and sisters, what are we really doing? What is our goal? Do we only care for plowing and sowing? Do we only care for preaching the gospel to save sinners? Do we only care for shepherding and feeding cattle? Do we only care to dispense food for the edification of the believers? Or are we satisfying the Lord with food and drink? The Lord is showing us here that after we come home we should not rest and be slothful. Although we are tired, we still need to endeavor to serve Him. Although we have worked much and suffered much, this cannot take the place of the ministering that He should receive. We need to forget all our experience and serve Him once again. But this is not to say that we do not need to eat. It merely means that our eating and drinking should come after the Lord's. We should also be filled and satisfied. Yet this should be after the Lord is filled and satisfied. We should also be happy. Yet this should be after the Lord's happiness. Therefore, let us ask ourselves to whom the glory of the work goes. Is everything that we are doing really for the satisfaction of the Lord's heart? Or is it for the satisfaction of our heart? Is the fruit of the labor for the Lord's satisfaction? Or is it for our own satisfaction? I deeply fear that many times the Lord has not gained anything, and yet we are satisfied. I deeply fear that many times before the Lord is happy, we are already very happy. We need to ask God to show us where we should stand in His presence and how we should really minister to Him in His presence.

Brothers and sisters, even if we do everything, we are nothing but useless servants. We are indeed very small.

Our goal and our striving are not the land and cattle, the world and the church. Our goal is the Lord. We are also striving for the Lord. He is our everything. Therefore, let us ask ourselves: Is the work we do truly for Christ, or is it only for sinners and brothers? Whoever can discern the difference between the ministry to sinners and the ministry to the Lord, and whoever can discern the difference between the ministry to the brothers and the ministry to the Lord, is blessed. In theory it seems easy to make such a distinction; yet to be able to inwardly distinguish the difference in our experience is a blessing. This kind of knowledge does not come easily. It requires the shedding of blood before the lesson can be learned. This kind of discernment is not easily apprehended. It requires many dealings before we can know it. Many times it requires the putting down of our life and the killing of our opinions before we can truly comprehend it. Ministering to the Lord is not as easy as ministering to the brothers and the sisters. Therefore, there is a vast difference between ministering to the Lord and ministering to the house.

Nevertheless, if the Holy Spirit works in us, it will not be that difficult for us to know. We need to ask the Lord to grant us grace, revelation, and light, so that we may see what ministering to Him means. A ministry to the sinners and a ministry to the Lord are two entirely different things; ministering to sinners is altogether different from ministering to the Lord. Brothers and sisters, sinners are not more important than the Lord. We need to ask the Lord to work on us, so that we will minister to Him. I cannot say anything more. I can only say that this is what the Lord wants to speak to us in these few days.